About the Author

Evy Y. Parkinson has been a professional clinical hypnotherapist, psychologist, mind-body transformational therapist, and teacher for over ten years. She has been living and experiencing her own unique spiritual path of growth and expansion, and the combination of these experiences and learning is what you will find in her writings. She was born and raised in Venezuela and emigrated to Trinidad and Tobago at the age of nineteen, where she then went away to study, live, and work in many other countries around the world. Evy considers herself a citizen of the world and a child of Mother Earth.

Drops of Wisdom

Evy Y. Parkinson

Drops of Wisdom

Olympia Publishers
London

www.olympiapublishers.com
OLYMPIA PAPERBACK EDITION

A CIP catalogue record for this title is available from the British Library.

ISBN: 978-1-83543-175-7

First Published in 2025

Olympia Publishers
Tallis House
2 Tallis Street
London
EC4Y 0AB

Printed in Great Britain

Dedication

I would like to dedicate this first book of poetry to my grandparents. Your wisdom and your love of books, novels, and poetry have been passed on to me, and this book would not exist if it weren't for each one of your influences. Lolo, Lola, Yoyo, and even though I did not meet my grandfather Richard, he has also passed on his influence energetically.

Acknowledgments

I thank my family for always being an unconditional support, and some of my closest friends who have helped me with their unconditional love and positive energy along this process.
I also want to thank the writers and authors who have had the courage to follow their hearts and pursue their writing dreams, no matter what. You have inspired and encouraged me to keep going.

PREFACE

How It All Started

When I was around eight years old and into my teens, my family and I used to go and visit my grandfather every week.

My grandfather's office in the house was more like a library. He used to collect newspapers, magazines, and stamps; he also loved books and literature.

There were so many books—old books whose pages were already yellowing. I remember the smell. I remember my feeling of total bliss just going into the office to look for the next book I wanted to borrow. Every week, I would take two or three and return them on the following visit.

The first books I ever read were on poetry. It was classical poetry, and I did not know half the words used, but I absolutely loved it because I felt the essence of the poem and made my own understanding. These early memories are imprinted in my being. For me, my grandfather's office was heaven, surrounded by books, that musty smell, and just getting lost as I stepped inside the narrative of each poem.

About this time, I also started writing, in Spanish since it is my first language, but I began learning English when I turned nineteen, and that eventually became the main language in which I wrote. It was not a conscious choice; it just happened.

Some of my first writings were in the form of poetry; at least that is how I think of them. I would just write down what I felt, using the vocabulary I had at the time.

In my teens, I started reading novels. I started borrowing

from my grandmothers then. Not romantic novels… suspense stories, crime novels, or tales about love and loss.

After I graduated from high school, I stopped for a while until I began reading self-help books, psychology, spirituality, and so on, which were the subjects I found most interesting at that point in my life and career. Fast-forward a few years, and I had completed my first book called "Mindful Eating: Connect with Your Body Through Awareness," a self-help book based on my personal and professional experience as a Mind-Body Therapist and Clinical Hypnotherapist.

My journey began in my grandfather's book-filled office, but even today, I feel the same way when I enter an old library or a big book store with all kinds of books. I am in heaven, and I feel I can stay there forever!

This book is written in the form of poetry. Apparently, I never stopped writing poems. I have been recording my thoughts and insights in a poetic form since an early age, and those notes and reflections have traveled with me over the years, added to right up to the present.

These poems are about healing, loss, pain, transformation, and love. I hope they bring you insights that you can relate to your personal life or help you on your own unique life path.

I have added some photography to the book, as I love taking pictures of Nature and I appreciate photography as an art.

Most pictures were taken by me, and a few of them were taken by my mother.

I hope you enjoy reading and going through this book.

It has been made with all my love.

HEALING

HEALING TAKES TIME

It cannot be rushed
It cannot be aggressively pushed
It cannot be dictated however your rational mind wishes to go
Healing is a gentle yet powerful process
It is a harmony between action and passivity, contraction and release
And IT has its OWN TIME.

THE MODERN WITCH

She senses your energy
She sees with more than her physical eyes
She will not respond to your physical looks…
She will respond to your intentions and hidden motivations.
She heals herself, thus she can heal others if they want it and allow it.
She will know what is in your mind, and she will know what is in your heart, but she will not judge you for any of it.
She will be compassionate and understanding.
She will be kind to your wounds.
But she is not dull or naive…
She has the strength of Nature
She will use the power of a hurricane if necessary.
She will know how to protect and defend herself if you have evil intentions toward her.
The pure-hearted will feel her love and healing energy. They will be forever touched by it.
Witches in the past were burned, silenced, shamed …
Witches today ARE NEEDED, ARE CALLED to BE who they are.
Witches today need empowerment.
The so-called witches from the past are the real healers today.

PAIN

If I keep avoiding acknowledging this pain,
How am I going to release it?
If I keep ignoring this pain,
How am I going to listen to what it has to say?
If I keep dishonoring what I feel,
How am I going to respect myself?
If I keep running from my deepest fears,
How am I going to meet them and befriend them?
If I keep closing my eyes so I don't have to see my wounds,
How am I going to heal them?

FROM THE EARTH

Flesh and bones
Blood and hair
We are made as animals on Earth.
We walk, we crawl, we swim, we move
We cry, we hurt, we love, we lust
We feel shame of our roots
We feel shame of our bodies
We feel shame of our animal nature
Calling it inferior
Trying to escape it
Trying to deny its needs and wants
because we are afraid of it
We have been taught to fear the beast inside
so the beast has become the master
The shame has won over, and so we hide our raw animal nature
And so that animal nature is not tamed, it is not handled with consciousness, care, acceptance, and love.
And so that animal nature becomes a violent beast controlled by fear
Controlled by the most basic impulses.
There is no master to tame the beast, the beast is loose and so it destroys everything on its way…
We have abandoned the beast
We have denied it and left it in the dark
We have become afraid of our own animal nature, and so it controls us
We forgot how to take care of our own beasts.

SIMPLICITY

We forget to listen to the breeze
We forget to listen to the ocean
We forget to listen to the birds…
We are too busy listening to our thoughts…

THE ILLUSION OF EGO

It is enough about getting caught up in the illusion…
It is enough.
It is enough about the self-inflicted suffering…
It is enough with the masochism.
We are not "saints" being martyrs…
Forget what you have been told, what you have been taught… it is not working.
How many times do you have to make the same mistake?
How strong is this addiction? How blind can one be?
And Nature stands on its own. Nature repairs itself. It is intelligent.
How I wish I was a tree…
And we worry about Nature. We want to take care of it…
Ignoring the real problem, using our creativity and intelligence to destroy…
To destroy the same Nature we are trying to "save."

YOU ARE ALREADY WHOLE

Like handicaps, we go on living; we go on walking…
With complete bodies, complete hearts, and complete brains…
We go on living like handicaps…
Limping… leaning on others… expecting someone else to give us what we need…
Begging for love…
Needing… getting what we can while we can…
Living life from lacking…
All we need is love…
All the love we need is within.

WHEN?

When will you realize that your uniqueness is in what you perceive as your "flaws"?
When will you be ready to know the real beauty that lies inside you?
When are you going to give yourself all the unconditional love and acceptance that you craved when you were a child?

BE LIKE A TREE

Grow your roots deep into the ground.
Stand tall and strong.
Let your neck and head be flexible
To the constant changes of the wind.

DISBELIEF

If you could only see what I see.
If you could only join me on this flight.
There is so much for everyone.
There is so much love and protection.
I am so sorry for ever doubting.

WHAT IF

But what happens if I try and I fail?
But what happens if I put my whole heart into it and it still doesn't work?
But what happens if it is all I've got and even that is not enough?
You need to trust the love you have for doing those things.
You need to trust it and let it be. Let it go. Let it flow.
If you don't, you will regret it.
If you don't, you will never know.

IN THE NAME OF LOVE

We were killing each other in the name of love.
Having some clear visions once in a while,
but slowly and progressively compromising our truths,
In the name of love.
Our intention was to keep the love,
but slowly and progressively, we paid more attention to keeping each other
to hold on to each other.
We became selfish in the name of love…
In the name of love
We started changing our priorities to make them fit in the private personal goal of having and keeping a relationship.
But thanks to losing each other, we found ourselves.
And in the name of love, we found love…

ENOUGH

I had it all, and I wasn't truly happy.
And is not that it wasn't enough.
Is that I thought that I was not enough.

THE REAL HEALER

The real healer cannot be bought.
The real healer isn't hypnotized by shiny, temporary things.
The real healer is here to do one job. That of guiding the person to find their own healing power within.
The real healer does not put her or his own personal egotistical gain before the wellbeing of the patient.
She or he does not put fame or money before what is best for the sick person.
The real healer is here to help you REMEMBER WHO you are.
The only drive of the healer is TO HEAL. Nothing else…

WOMAN

Woman, you are complex
You are WHOLE
You are so many things in one
You don't have to be either smart or sexy
Independent or nurturer
Beautiful or funny
A "lady" or a wild woman
You are ALL
You are the container for all of it, if you choose to.
You are a complex being; you don't have to fit in ONE box and deny all the other potentials.
You have the potential to develop all of your being.
To be a WHOLE WOMAN.
You have the strength and complexity of feeling so many different things at the same time.
You have the strength and complexity of feeling deeply and completely vulnerable to another being
And you have the strength and complexity to fight and risk your LIFE if necessary.

AWAKENING MAN

You are allowed to cry
You are allowed to fall
You are allowed to feel
You are allowed to scream
You are allowed to feel fear and sadness
You are a human being
You also feel
You also fear
You also fall
But you also learn
You are also strong
You are also courageous
You can also stand up again
You can also choose what is right over what is easy
You can also become a man of Honor
You can also be the true protector that you are meant to be
Have no shame in your tears
Have no shame of the guilt you feel
Because you feel
Because you care
Because you are meant to be whole
You are meant to be sensitive and strong
Supportive and protective
Forgive your past mistakes
Forgive because you wanted to do what was right
You thought you were doing what was right
But you didn't know how…

HUMAN

It is not the color of the skin
It is not the race
It is not the nationality
It is not the gender
It is not the social status
It is the quality of human being the individual chooses to be.

TRANSFORMATION

TRANSFORMATION

Life is a constant transformation.
We, as beings, have the ability to go with life and constantly transform,
But fear creeps in, and then we hold on to things, moments, and people.
Fear of "losing"
Losing is an illusion.
First, we never really lose anything that is really ours.
Second, what we are perceiving as losing is something that has been transformed into something else.
When something leaves our lives, there is always something else coming to fill that space that will complement your life and support who you are becoming in a better way
If we allow the space
If we allow the flow
If we open our minds to endless possibilities and relax…
If we let go and trust…

WOUNDS

These wounds that I had to heal
These scars that I carry in my heart
Are the ones that have made me feel so deeply
They have made me go to the core of my being
They have made me as authentic and real as I can possibly be
They have helped me embrace my vulnerability, my humanity
They have helped me to be more compassionate toward myself and others
These scars that I carry in my heart
Have made me more resilient
They have become the roadmap of my wisdom…

POTENTIAL

Fly high
The highest you know you can,
each day
And the right ones will join you in that fly
To fly freely and joyfully.
The right company will fly as high as they know they can
They will rise to join you.
The wrong company will want and try to pull you down,
So you can stay with them on the ground.

CONNECTION

Sometimes we'll walk with company, and sometimes we'll walk alone.
We all walk at different speeds, and that's okay; perhaps we'll meet at another point in time
and we catch up for a while…
I love you, so I want you to go at your own speed, at your own pace…
We are not in a race.
We are simply moving—constantly moving.
And even if we are in different places, we can still hear each other,
We can still feel each other,
We remain connected by this inexplicable force.

RELEASING

Those ghosts from the past will hold on as long as they can
They will hold on as hard as they can
And they will stay as long as we give them something to hold on to.
They are known to us
They are familiar
in a way they represent "love" for us
They were our home once.
But that home no longer serves us,
That home no longer serves the new you, the parts of you that are growing.

RAW

I am wild
I am raw
I can be dirty
And untamed
But I can also be soft and tamed
Settled and relaxed
In a home that is full of warmth
I am both at the same time
I can be untamed and tamed at the same time
Because I know I am wild and free on the inside.

GROWTH

When you feel rejected,
You have an opportunity to accept yourself.
When you feel left out,
You have an opportunity to welcome yourself.
When you feel abandoned,
You have an opportunity to hold yourself.
When you feel lonely,
You have an opportunity to give yourself company.
When you feel challenged,
You have an opportunity to grow.
When you feel hurt,
You have an opportunity to heal.

ENCOUNTERS

There are some people that you meet, and they touch your heart as soon as you meet them
and that touch stays forever.
There are some people that you will meet and will hurt you so deeply that will break any walls you ever built around your heart.
You will meet others that will just bring joy and play into your life, reminding you not to take life so seriously.
There will be people who "look" beautiful on the outside
but have forgotten their inner light
and you will meet others
who are beautiful inside and out.
Others will pass through your life like a fresh breeze, leaving you wishing for more of that breeze,
Teaching you not to hold on to anyone or any situation
because you don't know what life has stored for you.

THE WHEEL

I am the Angel
And the Devil
I am the rapist
And the rapped
I am the oppressor
And the oppressed
I am the ignorant
And the wise
I am the bad
And the good
I am the vessel for hate and love
For fear and courage
For greediness and sharing
I contain everything, and everything contains me.
We are the universe, seeing ourselves as separate things…

SUCCESSFUL

Real success in life
Is going to sleep every night
With your conscience clean
And your heart at peace.

LIFE

Everything changes
Life is like the tide of the sea
It goes up and down
Sometimes we have, and sometimes we don't have
The tide is changing all the time
It moves
Sometimes we have and sometimes we don't have
It goes up and down
Everything moves
Sometimes we are high, and sometimes we are low
We are constantly moving and changing.

CHANNELING

I am the lion, and the lioness.
I am the snake transmuting and transforming the energy.
I channel her power for constant transformation and renewal.
I become the butterfly light and beautiful.
I harness the power of the eagle, who sees and flies high.
I become the hummingbird light, intelligent, joyful, and skillful.
I am the wild and the tamed horse
The one that runs freely and the one that stays home.
I am the lion, and the lioness.
Empowered, whole, focused, grounded
With no concern for what any other animal is doing.

FLOWERING

Each flower is different and beautiful on its own.
Each one is unique in every sense, yet they are all flowers.
Each one of us was born with a unique seed within.
It's up to each one of us to nurture, water, and take care of its growth.
If we are curious and free enough to see what flower we are meant to become.

SELF-DISCOVERY

What if your greatest gifs are hidden behind that dark cave you are so afraid to walk in?
What if your greatest treasures are hidden right inside that darkness that you are so afraid of?
What if your greatest strength is your vulnerability?
What would happen if you dared to feel with your whole heart?
What would happen if you allowed your feelings to flow?
What would happen if you gave everything you had from your soul and your heart in each moment? With no reservations

EGO

Feeling superior to… or
Feeling inferior to…
Two sides of the same coin
The Endless Ego Game

THE PHOENIX

And from the ashes
The phoenix raises.
Majestic, stronger than ever before
Once more…

LOVE

Photo by Richard Parkinson

Photo by Amenaida Miralles

HEART TO HEART

I see you
I feel you
You are also tied down by the fears of the mind.
By the many self-doubts the mind carries.
You too want to express your deepest feelings, your truth, your beauty, your gifts, without restrictions.
You are free. You are wild, that's your Nature.
You want to open your wings and fly, flowing with the wind, simply flowing with life.
I can see you
I can feel you
You are one of those who dream, who are sensitive, who feel the pain of the world.
That is why the mind has created so many walls to protect you from getting hurt again.
But you don't care. You just want to feel, to express, to give, to love, to keep expanding and being light.
You have been hurt before, you have been broken before, you have been taken for granted before….
But you don't care…
You have only become stronger and bigger from those wounds… from healing and putting those parts together… because each time you needed more love to put those pieces together… and you grew wiser.
The mind and the ego don't know.

Their job is to make sure you never go through any other pain or betrayal again.
But keeping yourself repressed, keeping yourself tied down, and silenced is no life at all…

LOVING YOURSELF

It is easy to love yourself when you are succeeding
It's easy to love yourself when you feel your prettiest
It's easy to love yourself when you feel you are at your "perfect weight" or "perfect body"
It's easy to love yourself when you have people around telling you how much they love you or like you…
But what happens when you are falling down?
When you feel your ugliest?
When you got some extra kilos?
When you are feeling down and lonely?
When you feel rejected or as an outsider?
When you feel your weakest?
Who loves you then?
How do you treat yourself in those moments?
How do you practice kindness, understanding, and compassion with yourself?
What kind of friend are you to yourself in those moments?
You know LOVE when you start embracing ALL OF YOU.
The WHOLE YOU.
The darkness and the light.
When you are your best and most supportive friend in the hardest times of your life
When you can hold all those wounded parts that you find in you with the same care and deep love you would hold a wounded puppy…

LOVE

"Love is blind," they say…
Love is not blind… real love anyway…
Real love is seeing the truth
It is seeing all aspects of something or someone.
It is seeing the dark and the light and embracing the WHOLE.
It is diving deep into what is unseen by others…
Real love is REAL
REAL means:
No masks, no pretending, no hiding, no games
It does not manipulate.
It does not demand that you abandon parts of your true self.
It means being your whole self.
It means feeling free to be who you truly are in each step of the way…
and this is real lasting love.

LEARNING TO LOVE

When you feel compassion, you are loving
When you forgive, you are loving
When you trust, you are loving
When you accept, you are loving
When you give, just give—not trade—you are loving
When you are honest, you are loving
When you are understanding, you are loving
When you are at peace with yourself, that is love

FREE

I own nothing, and nothing owns me.
I am free.
I do not own you. You do not own me.
I do not own anything. I am not owned by
anything or anyone.
You are free. I am free.
You are free to be next to me. I am free to be next to you.
You are free to stay, and you are free to go.
I love you, so I want you to feel free.
I love watching you being you.
I enjoy you. I do not own you.
Love me. Appreciate me.
Do not desire to own me.

HOW?

How wouldn't I want the best for you?
How wouldn't I wish you to be and have everything you want?
How couldn't I want you to have the life you choose to have?
if you are the person I love the most in this world.
How wouldn't I want you to be free?

DID YOU KNOW?

Did you know that your worth has nothing to do with what anyone else thinks of you?
Did you know that your worth is independent of what happens or doesn't happen in your life?
Do you know that only you can find your own worth?
That your worth is and has always been in you?
That you are worthy because you are here.
You are worthy of this life.
You are worthy of your life.
You are worthy of love. You are worthy of your love…

THANK YOU

Thank you,
Thank you for crossing my path…
Thank you for your part in my way…
Thank you for your energy
Thank you for your inspiration
Thank you for your softness
Thank you for what you have given me
Thank you for helping me know myself better.

NICE TO MEET YOU

It was a pleasure to meet you.
It was beautiful to watch you being you.
Knowing that it was just for a moment that our paths were crossing,
Our eyes understood.
My heart needed a little more time to let go.

TOO SOON

But it was too soon
It was too soon for us
It was too much to handle
We were too immature to appreciate what we felt
What we saw
What we encountered
It was too soon to hug
It was too soon to feel each other's hearts by pressing our chests together
It was too much to handle
And we were too young to understand
And I do not know if you ever felt the same again
I know I haven't
I know it remains in my whole being
Still without an explanation
No reason
No logic
Just the experience planted in my being

Photo by Denise Speck

WHEN I LET GO

When I let go
Is when I feel the most empowered.
When I let you go
Wanting you to be free to choose
Is when I feel most secure and empowered.
Because I want you to want me on your own
I want you to choose me on your own
I want a man who decides for himself.
I would not want to decide for you.
So I let you go
I set you free every time I miss you.
Every time, I want to hold you and keep you by my side forever.
No matter how much I want it
I remember that I have me.
I have my heart and my love first and always.
That I have all this love here for me
And for you, if you choose to receive it from me.
I let you go
I let you fly
I let you Be
There is no bigger love than the one that is free
Is completely free to be, to go, to leave
But still chooses to stay.
Knowing that you are still free

Still free to choose…
I have all this love and warmth here in my heart
And I am open to share it
To welcome you into my life, my world, my home.
So I release the desire to control
I release the fear that you will fly away
That I will never see you or feel you ever again.
I am Here
I am Love
I am Fulfilled
I am Whole
… and I can feel you in my heart
Here and always…

WHEN I SAW YOU

I just knew when I saw you.
I don't know what I knew.
I just knew it was something New.

JOY

When you experience without judgement,
Then you experience with freedom,
Experiencing with freedom is Joy.

Photo by Denise Speck

ONE LOOK

One look was enough.
One deep, honest look into your eyes was enough
To see purity, to see innocence.
One silent, clear look into your eyes to know that I have never seen that before.
That what I felt was real. No need for words. No need for touch.
One deep, honest look was enough to touch my soul.
One silent look made time stop.
There was silence, emptiness, purity, eternity, innocence, love.
That one deep, honest look will keep traveling with me as long as I live.

LION

A lion knows he is a lion.
He does not need to prove that he is a lion.
He IS a lion.
He doesn't need to show off.
He doesn't need to prove anything.
He is a leader.
He leads with
Honor. Majesty. Wisdom.
Strength and power.
Protector of his family.
Loving. Sweet. Playful. Relaxed with his pack.
Trusting.
He is a lion…
He does not need to prove that he is a lion
He knows that *he is a lion*
And he bows…
A true leader.
He helps, protects, and supports the wellbeing of his pack.
He knows that he is part of it.
He does not see them as slaves.
He does not abuse them.
He leads from his heart.
The Heart of a Lion.

AN ANGEL

One of my greatest teachers
You were full of pure love
You were full of strength.
You taught me how unbelievably strong and how unbelievably fragile we can be at the same time.
You had one of the biggest and most uplifting spirits I have ever met.
Time and time again, you surprised me with some unexpected level of strength and joy.
You have been the most stubborn being I have ever met
And that stubbornness made you into that unshakable presence standing by my side,
always…
I did not know the magnitude of your love and presence in my life until you were gone
And there was an undeniable open space left.
But you will always live in me; you have become part of me, and you live in my heart each second and in each breath I take.
And you didn't leave until I was prepared to let you go…
But no matter how prepared we are, we never feel ready.
We cannot grasp the experience, and how challenging it can be, and how much of an emotional roller coaster it can be until we are IN IT.
You are one of my biggest love stories in this life
You taught me unconditional love

You taught me compassion
You taught me patience
You showed me that when something is meant to be in your life, IT IS.
If it leaves, it will always come back.
My love,
There was a reason why your name was Angel.
My Angel.

THE PATH OF LOVE

The path of love is NOT only roses and romantic illusions.
The path of love will transform you.
It will take you through the darkest places in your being.
It will show you everything that is not love.
And you will see it, feel it, experience it… to know what is not love.
As you learn what is not love, you equally learn what IS…
The path of love is tough sometimes, is rough sometimes
It shakes you when you are falling asleep, it pushes you when you are becoming lazy, and helps you rest when you need to rest and recharge…
But it's all LOVE. Loving is not easy.
Hating is easy, being hurt and resentful is easy, choosing separation is easy, judging is easy.
Try loving… that is hard…
Try loving the world when you see the behaviors that you see.
Try loving yourself when you are carrying so much pain and beliefs of not being good enough. Beliefs that you are not accepted, that you have no place here, that you are not worthy, that you are not loved…
If you follow the path of love
If you allow it to transform you
You will free yourself from those beliefs.
You will realize how loved you truly are.
You will realize that you are love itself.

LETTER TO SELF

I still love myself, even if I make the same mistake.
Even if I fall with the same stone again, I still love myself.
I know I am learning. I know I am growing.
And I still love myself, even if I get angry at the world and at myself.
Even when I hurt myself, I still love myself. I feel compassion for myself because I know this is no easy life.
It is not easy to be a human at this time; it is very hard to stay sane when you are around madness. When there are shadows everywhere and you feel so deeply.
I still love myself even if I get lost in that shadow, even if I forget who I am for a while.
I still love myself.
I release myself from blame.
Blame toward myself for being human, for feeling so deeply, for making mistakes, for falling down and trying again… for not giving up … because it is so much easier to give up.
For continuing to get up and face life again and again, no matter how much I have already been through.
I free myself from guilt.
I free myself from blame.
I release everything that I have picked up on the way that does not belong to me.
As I release it, I get back to the truth that I am already free.
that I was born free
and that I have always been free.